Reagan's Romps

Reagan's Romps

Poems by

Brenda Kay Ledford

Cover design byShay Culligan

ISBN: 978-1-952326-87-5

Kelsay Books
502 South 1040 East, A-119
American Fork, Utah, 84003

Acknowledgments

Angels of Heaven & Earth: "Reagan's Rain Boots:

Blue Ridge Poet Blogspot: "Grandpa Randy"

Pancakes in Heaven: "Reagan Blanche"

Pinesong (NC Poetry Society)*:* "Flying Squirrel"

Red Plank House: "Reagan's Rain Boots"

SHEMOM: "Reagan Blanche"

West End Poet's Newsletter: "Flying Squirrel"

Contents

Reagan Blanche

You could not wait
until April to burst forth
and to proclaim your worth,
spring beckoned your birth.

Jonquils dotted the hillsides
with churned butter,
the season of life,
you could not wait.

Like the lambs
frolicking through the verdant grass,
my great-niece would not wait
until April to burst forth.

Tender pink skin,
an angel sent from heaven,
you broke forth
and proclaimed your worth.

Rain Boots

Tap, tap, tap!
A steady drumbeat
on the tin roof.

Orange rain boots
splash, splash, splashing
through the mud puddles.

Cute little girl,
blonde curls flying,
parading in orange.

Raindrops tapping
the red-plank house,
Reagan wearing her rain boots.

Owl-O-Ween

Taking a hayride
through the pumpkin patch,
corn shocks rattle their fingers.

Leaves whirl on the wind,
sipping hot apple cider,
taking a hayride.

Scarecrows jitterbug,
an owl hoots in the oak,
through the pumpkin patch.

Trick-or-treaters scamper
beneath a Harvest Moon,
corn shocks rattle their fingers.

Boo-A-Teen

At Halloween
a black-and-white cat
perches on the fence,

peeks through Reagan's window.
He slinks over a carpet of leaves,
circles the red-plank house,

hunting in the fog.
A covey of blue jays fly,
short of his paws.

Foliage floats on mud puddles
like a mural of watercolors,
little goblins don their raingear.

Merry Bear-y Bear

Reagan's coming!
Hurry! Hurry! Hurry!
Make the merry bear-y.

Gather felt, buttons, and filling,
cut out the pattern.
Reagan's coming.

No time to waste,
Christmas is coming.
Hurry! Hurry! Hurry!

Little Teddy bear,
a present for Reagan.
Make the Christmas bear!

Christmas Presents

Little hands rip paper
from the Christmas presents,
Reagan jumps up and down with glee.

Decorations sparkle on the tree,
surprises tumble from boxes,
little hands rip paper.

The adults laugh and clap,
a puppy sings merry tunes
from the Christmas presents.

For awhile peace reigns,
we celebrate with childish eyes,
Reagan jumps up and down with glee.

Song of the Red Bird

Listen to the song
of the red bird perched
on the highest branch
of the holly tree:
the east wind tosses
her dress and feathers,
tilting her head
to the snowflakes twirling
across the woods,
the Red Bird trills,
"Cheer! Cheer! Cheer!"
on the grayest day
of the new year,
she does not hear
the other creatures
complaining and shivering
in the cold winter,
the Red Bird keeps
a cheerful song in her heart,
and bobs as she tweets!

Polar Bears

Near the Arctic Circle,
polar bears roam the tundra,
master of the food chain,
whales leap in the Hudson Bay.

Seals slide on the ice,
bears gorge blubber,
males wrestle for dominance,
two thousand pounds of power.

A parka of fur,
charcoal eyes sparkle,
resisting the urge to pet,
left paw crushes the prey.

White bears of the North
lumber free as snowflakes,
the aurora lights flicker,
broccoli streaks across the sky.

Flying Squirrel

Fly flyflyfly
  fly
    through the trees

fly flyflyfly
  fly
    to the hills

find walnuts
  hickory nuts
     acorns corn

gather plenty
gather plenty
fly   flyflyfly

scamper
  sail
    somersault

fly flyflyfly
    winter's coming

Dusting Powders

The winter is here
and the wind blows,
dusting powders fly like snow.

Children at their play,
Reagan's new tricycle,
the winter is here.

The bees are asleep in their hives,
a Teddy bear sings merry tunes,
and the wind blows.

Dressing by the fireplace,
dipping into the *Wind Song,*
dusting powders fly like snow.

Great-Grandma Bea's House

Over the mountains
and through the woods
to Grandma Bea's house
for the holidays.

Over the Blue Ridge Mountains,
beside Lake Chatuge,
far back in the Clay County
to Grandma's house we go.

Over the Interstate,
around mountain roads,
hairpin curves, spinning, cliffs;
how much further to Grandma's?

Over the mountains
and through the woods,
hugs and kisses welcome
me to Grandma Bea's house.

Books

Sitting in Grandma's lap,
looking and touching picture books,
animals make funny sounds.

The cow goes, "Moo! Moo! Moo!"
"Quack! Quack! Quack!" says the duck.
Sitting in Grandma's lap.

"Meow," to you says the cat.
"Wolf! Wolf! Wolf!" barks the dog.
Looking and touching picture books.

The sheep, "Baa-baa-baa!"
Piggy goes, "Oink! Oink! Oink!"
Animals make funny sounds.

Grandpa Randy

Grandpa Randy is dandy,
he plays with me,
makes funny faces,
he's a funny grandpa.

He plays with me,
Grandpa snorts like a horse,
he's a funny grandpa,
we are two playmates.

Grandpa snorts like a horse,
it's fun to visit dandy Randy,
we are two playmates,
he's a funny Grandpa!

He puts paper on his head,
makes funny faces,
trots and snorts like a horse;
Grandpa Randy is dandy!

Coloring

Peeling back the paper,
Reagan breaks them to pieces
and makes more crayons!

Prry! Pra-lang! POP! POP!
Crayons filling her box,
peeling back the paper.

Marking in the coloring book,
she stays inside the lines,
Reagan breaks crayons to pieces.

Mommy's little artist,
break, break, break;
and making more crayons!

Telephone

Call Brenda and Grandma Bea!
Reagan loves to talk on the telephone.
Maybe when she grows up,
little girl will be an operator!

Ring, ding, ring, ding!
Merrily sings the phone.
It's time to talk,
no time for a walk.

Call Brenda and Grandma Bea!
Go ahead and talk Reagan.
"How are you Brenda and Bea?"
So the telephone rings, sings, and dings!

My Valentine

If dogs were doodle bugs,
and strawberries were lemons,
and the tulip
had another flower,
if bears were rocks,
I would love my great-niece,
little Reagan Blanche
just the same,
even if she had
another name!

Song of the Rain Crow

In the poplar tree,
I sing for the mountains.

The blue-green grasses,
I sing for the streams.

In the cotton clouds,
I sing for the rain.

The pretty flowers,
I sing for them.

In the poplar tree,
I sing for rain.

I sing for rain!

Horseback Riding

The painted pony
prance, prance, prances
through the blue-green grass.

"Come, little Reagan,
let's take a ride," says
the painted pony.

Through the woods
and fields of Wilmore;
prance, prance, prance.

The painted pony
and Reagan riding
through the blue-green grass.

Pepper the Pig

Once Pepper the Pig
sat upon a hall.
No! No! I mean a wall.

Pepper the Pig
tried to fall.
No! No! I mean call.

Pepper the Pig
tried to call
her daddy and mommy.

Pepper the Pig
fell off the wall
she feared she got broke.

Pepper the Pig
sat upon a hall,
no wall, and called her parents.

The Clock

Tick-tock! Tick-Tock!
Not a sound
but the clock.

Reagan lies in bed
waiting to get up.
Tick-tock! Tick-tock!

Tick-tock! Tick-Tock!
The alarm booms,
shakes the room!

Tick-tock! Tick-tock!
Time for breakfast.
Bring Grandpa's Cheerios!

Oh, Grandma,
bring the strawberries, too.
Tick-tock goes the clock.

Hyacinth

"Come, come, come,
outside and play today,"
sings merry Miss Sunshine.

"No, it's too cold,"
says the little Hyacinth.
"I'm not that bold."

"Come, come, come,
we'll have a lot of fun
running in the sun."

"No, I'll freeze my nose,"
says the little Hyacinth.
"I'll stay in bed today."

Sunshine shakes her head.
Miss Hyacinth pokes
out of the ground to play all day.

Mr. Turtle

There was a turtle.
He was quite shy.
He hid in a shell.
He fell into a pool.

Turt was green, green.
Turt took his time.
Turt bathed in sunshine.

Turt nipped at a spider.
Turt nipped at an ant.
Turt nipped at a leaf.
Turt nipped at a bee.

Turt ate the spider.
Turt ate the ant.
Turt ate the bee.
But he didn't eat Reagan.

Rabbit

Reagan runs like a rabbit.
Hop! Hop! Hop!
She stops for a rest.

Beside the brook,
rabbit sits in the green-blue grass,
he lifts his ears

and hears the waters
singing, "Spring is coming."
He twitches his nose

and munches the grass
for his lunch.
Yum! Yum! Yum!

The Little Leprechauns

There were some leprechauns
where the shamrocks leap.
They slid down a rainbow

and splashed in gold.
They danced with glee
because you see

they found a pot of gold
at the end of the rainbow.
After an Irish rain,

the little men sang
and wished little Reagan
Happy St. Paddy Day!

Butterflies

Fairy of the flowers
with wings of spun glass,
you flit about the grass,
and land on Reagan's hand.

Small pearls in the poplars,
honeysuckle perfumes a breeze,
the gaudy commodore zigzagging,
fairy of the flowers.

Drinking the marigold's mystery,
there are jewels on your body,
you flutter in the air
with wings like spun glass.

When the wild roses ripen
in the Blue Ridge Mountains,
and the rain crow lifts songs,
you flit about the flowers.

Frogs

You know it's spring.
The creek is echoing:
Croak! Croak! Croak!

You know it's spring.
The mountains are resounding:
bullfrogs blow their trumpets.

You know it's spring.
Hyatt-Mill Creek is
holding a musical.

You know it's spring.
Wood frogs, green frogs, bullfrogs
Croak! Croak! Croak!

The Cows

The black and white cows
moo, moo, moo,
in the green-blue grass.

They give milk
to soak Reagan's cereal,
and build strong bones.

The pretty cows
chew their cuds
on the Kentucky farms.

The black and white cows
wander, ponder, fonder through
the clover fields moo, mooing!

The Giraffe

Far away in Africa,
a tall, tall, tall
animal towers above
the other animals.

The giraffe gallops
over the grasslands,
reaches her long neck
to the tree tops,

nibbles leaves, twigs,
and fruit from the trees.
Her coat patterns
are like puzzle pieces.

She sleeps standing up,
the creatures look up
to this giant:
queen of the grasslands.

The Lion

When the lion heart roars,
the grasslands tremble,
little creatures run.

When the lion heart roars,
all the animals
leave him alone.

The grasslands are his throne,
he rules the land,
he's louder than a band.

When the lion heart roars,
his soft plush fur
and heart-shaped mane

beg to be hugged.
The lion heart's roar
is a-roar-able!

Animals Touch Screens

Paws touch the screen,
beaks peck the screen,
noses touch the screen.

Touch screens.
Animals touch the screens.
Animals love screens.

Penguins peck screens.
A wolf noses screens.
A lion paws screens.

Turtle taps the screen.
Monkey pats the screen.
Leopard chases the mouse.

Touch screens.
Curious animals
love the touch screens.

About the Author

Author, poet and blogger Brenda Kay Ledford, is a retired educator. She received her Master of Arts in Early Childhood Education from Western Carolina University and studied Journalism at the University of Tennessee. She holds a diploma of highest honors in Creative Writing from the Stratford Career Institute.

She's former editor of *Tri-County Communicator* at Tri-County Community College and previous reporter for the *Smoky Mountain Sentinel*. She received an award from the North Carolina Press Association for her feature on the John C. Campbell Folk School.

Ledford belongs to the North Carolina Writer's Network, North Carolina Poetry Society, Ridgeline Literary Alliance, Georgia Poetry Society, and a charter member of the Byron Herbert Reece Society. She's listed with *A Directory of American Poets and Fiction Writers, North Carolina Literary Map,* and received the 2019 Marquis Who's Who in America Lifetime Achievement Award for writing and as an educator.

Her work has appeared in many journals including "Lyricist," "The Broad River Review," "Pembroke Magazine," "Asheville Poetry Review," "Wild Goose Poetry Review," "Town Creek Poetry," "Appalachian Heritage," "Journal of Kentucky Studies," "Our State," "Byron Herbert Reece Website," "Our State," "Chicken Soup for the Soul," "Angels on Earth," 40 Old Mountain Press anthologies, and many other publications.

Aldrich Press published two poetry books: *Crepe Roses* and *Red Plank House.* She received the Paul Green Multimedia Award from North Carolina Society of Historians for these books. Ledford has won the Paul Green Award a dozen times for her books, blogs, and collecting oral history on Southern Appalachia.

Ledford give poetry readings throughout the Southeast and has taught creative writing at the John C. Campbell Folk School and for workshops. She's appeared on "The Blue Sky Show" on WJUL/WJRB Radio Station and read poetry on "The Common Cup," on Windstream Communications Cable Television. Her interview appeared on the City Lights Bookstore in Sylva, NC on their Podcast. Clay County, NC Chamber of Commerce interviewed Ledford on YouTube and she appeared on "The Chamber Commerce" on Windstream Cable TV.

She has studied poetry under Karen Paul Holmes, Dr. Will Wright, Dr. Michael Dietrich, Dr. Scott Owens, Dr. Bettie Sellers, Dr. Ted Olson, Dr. Steve Harvey, Dr. Robert Brewer, Katherine Stripling Byer, Nancy Simpson, Dr. Catherine Carter, Dr. Celia H. Miles, Maureen Ryan Griffin, former North Carolina Poet Laureate Dr. Shelby Stephenson, and Richard Krawiec.

www.ingramcontent.com/pod-product-compliance
Lightning Source LLC
Chambersburg PA
CBHW071359090426
42738CB00012B/3177